The Coming Community

Edited by

Sandra Buckley

Michael Hardt

Brian Massumi

THEORY OUT OF BOUNDS

...UNCONTAINED

BY

THE

DISCIPLINES,

INSUBORDINATE...

PRACTICES OF RESISTANCE

...Inventing,

excessively,

In the between...

PROCESSES

OF

HYBRIDIZATION

The Coming Community

Giorgio
Agamben

Translated by Michael Hardt

Theory out of Bounds   *Volume 1*

University of Minnesota Press

Minneapolis • London

ISBN 0-8166-2235-3 (pbk.)

Published by the University of Minnesota Press
111 Third Avenue South, Suite 290, Minneapolis, MN 55401-2520
http://www.upress.umn.edu

Printed in the United States of America on acid-free paper

Contents

Translator's Acknowledgments

The translator

would like to thank Brian Massumi, Mike Sullivan, and Giorgio Agamben

for their generous assistance

in the preparation of this translation.

Whatever

THE COMING being is whatever[1] being. In the Scholastic enumeration of transcendentals (*quodlibet ens est unum, verum, bonum seu perfectum* — whatever entity is one, true, good, or perfect), the term that, remaining unthought in each, conditions the meaning of all the others is the adjective *quodlibet*. The common translation of this term as "whatever" in the sense of "it does not matter which, indifferently" is certainly correct, but in its form the Latin says exactly the opposite: *Quodlibet ens* is not "being, it does not matter which," but rather "being such that it always matters." The Latin always already contains, that is, a reference to the will (*libet*). Whatever being has an original relation to desire.

The Whatever in question here relates to singularity not in its indifference with respect to a common property (to a concept, for example: being red, being French, being Muslim), but only in its being *such as it is*. Singularity is thus freed from the false dilemma that obliges knowledge to choose between the ineffability of the individual and the intelligibility of the universal. The intelligible, according to a beautiful expression of Levi ben Gershon (Gersonides), is neither a universal nor an individual included in a series, but rather "singularity insofar as it is whatever singularity." In this conception, such-and-such being is reclaimed from its having this or that property, which identifies it as belonging to this or that set, to this or that class (the reds, the French, the Muslims) — and it is reclaimed not for another class nor for the simple generic absence of any belonging, but for its being-*such*, for belonging itself. Thus being-*such*, which remains constantly hidden in the condition of belonging ("there is an *x such that* it belongs to *y*") and which is in no way a real predicate, comes to light itself: The singularity exposed as such is whatever you *want*, that is, lovable.

Love is never directed toward this or that property of the loved one (being blond, being small, being tender, being lame), but neither does it neglect the properties in favor of an insipid generality (universal love): The lover wants the loved one *with all of its predicates*, its being such as it is. The lover desires the *as* only insofar as it is *such* — this is the lover's particular fetishism. Thus, whatever singularity (the Lovable) is never the intelligence of some thing, of this or that quality or essence, but only the intelligence of an intelligibility. The movement Plato describes as erotic anamnesis is the movement that transports the object not toward another thing or another place, but toward its own taking-place — toward the Idea.

From Limbo

WHERE DO whatever singularities come from? What is their realm? Saint Thomas's questions about limbo contain the elements for a response. According to Saint Thomas, the punishment of unbaptized children who die with no other fault than original sin cannot be an afflictive punishment, like that of hell, but only a punishment of privation that consists in the perpetual lack of the vision of God. The inhabitants of limbo, in contrast to the damned, do not feel pain from this lack: Since they have only natural and not supernatural knowledge, which is implanted in us at baptism, they do not know that they are deprived of the supreme good, or, if they do know (as others claim) they cannot suffer from it more than a reasonable person is pained by the fact that he or she cannot fly. If they were to feel pain they would be suffering from a penalty for which they could not make amends and thus their pain would end up leading them into hopelessness, like the damned. This would not be just. Moreover, their bodies, like those of the blessed, cannot be affected; they are impassible. But this is true only with respect to the action of divine justice; in every other respect they fully enjoy their natural perfection.

The greatest punishment—the lack of the vision of God—thus turns into a natural joy: Irremediably lost, they persist without pain in divine abandon. God has not forgotten them, but rather they have always already forgotten God; and in the face of their forgetfulness, God's forgetting is impotent. Like letters with no addressee, these uprisen beings remain without a destination. Neither blessed like the elected, nor hopeless like the damned, they are infused with a joy with no outlet.

This nature of limbo is the secret of Robert Walser's world. His creatures are irreparably astray, but in a region that is beyond perdition and salvation: Their nullity, of which they are so proud, is principally a neutrality with respect to salvation—the most radical objection that has ever been levied against the very idea of redemption. The truly unsavable life is the one in which there is nothing to save, and against this the powerful theological machine of Christian *oiconomia* runs aground. This is what leads to the curious mixture of rascality and humility, of cartoon-style thoughtlessness and minute scrupulousness that characterizes Walser's characters; this is what leads, also, to their ambiguity, so that every relationship with them seems always on the verge of ending up in bed: It is neither pagan *hubris* nor animal timidity, but simply the impassibility of limbo with respect to divine justice.

Like the freed convict in Kafka's *Penal Colony*, who has survived the destruction of the machine that was to have executed him, these beings have left the world of guilt and justice behind them: The light that rains down on them is that irreparable light of the dawn following the *novissima dies* of judgment. But the life that begins on earth after the last day is simply human life.

III

Example

THE ANTINOMY of the individual and the universal has its origin in language. The word "tree" designates all trees indifferently, insofar as it posits the proper universal significance in place of singular ineffable trees (*terminus supponit significatum pro re*). In other words, it transforms singularities into members of a class, whose meaning is defined by a common property (the condition of belonging ε). The fortune of set theory in modern logic is born of the fact that the definition of the set is simply the definition of linguistic meaning. The comprehension of singular distinct objects m in a whole M is nothing but the name. Hence the inextricable paradoxes of classes, which no "beastly theory of types" can pretend to solve. The paradoxes, in effect, define the place of linguistic being. Linguistic being is a class that both belongs and does not belong to itself, and the class of all classes that do not belong to themselves is language. Linguistic being (being-called) is a set (the tree) that is at the same time a singularity (*the* tree, *a* tree, *this* tree); and the mediation of meaning, expressed by the symbol ε, cannot in any way fill the gap in which only the article succeeds in moving about freely.

One concept that escapes the antinomy of the universal and the particular has long been familiar to us: the example. In any context where it exerts its force, the example is characterized by the fact that it holds for all cases of the same type, and, at the same time, it is included among these. It is one singularity among others, which, however, stands for each of them and serves for all. On one hand, every example is treated in effect as a real particular case; but on the other, it remains understood that it cannot serve in its particularity. Neither particular nor universal, the example is a singular object that presents itself as such, that *shows* its singularity. Hence the pregnancy of the Greek term, for example: *para-deigma*, that which is shown alongside (like the German *Bei-spiel*, that which plays alongside). Hence the proper place of the example is always beside itself, in the empty space in which its undefinable and unforgettable life unfolds. This life is purely linguistic life. Only life in the word is undefinable and unforgettable. Exemplary being is purely linguistic being. Exemplary is what is not defined by any property, except by being-called. Not being-red, but being-*called*-red; not being-Jakob, but being-*called*-Jakob defines the example. Hence its ambiguity, just when one has decided to take it really seriously. Being-called—the property that establishes all possible belongings (being-called-Italian, -dog, -Communist)—is also what can bring them all back radically into question. It is the Most Common that cuts off any real community. Hence the impotent omnivalence of whatever being. It is neither apathy nor promiscuity nor resignation. These pure singularities communicate only in the empty space of the example, without being tied by any common property, by any identity. They are expropriated of all identity, so as to appropriate belonging itself, the sign ε. Tricksters or fakes, assistants or 'toons, they are the exemplars of the coming community.

IV

Taking Place

THE MEANING of ethics becomes clear only when one understands that the good is not, and cannot be, a good thing or possibility beside or above every bad thing or possibility, that the authentic and the true are not real predicates of an object perfectly analogous (even if opposed) to the false and the inauthentic.

Ethics begins only when the good is revealed to consist in nothing other than a grasping of evil and when the authentic and the proper have no other content than the inauthentic and the improper. This is the meaning of the ancient philosophical adage according to which "veritas patefacit se ipsam et falsum." Truth cannot be shown except by showing the false, which is not, however, cut off and cast aside somewhere else. On the contrary, according to the etymology of the verb *patefacere*, which means "to open" and is linked to *spatium*, truth is revealed only by giving space or giving a place to non-truth—that is, as a taking-place of the false, as an exposure of its own innermost impropriety.

As long as the authentic and the good had a separate place among humans (they took *part*), life on earth was certainly infinitely more beautiful (still today we know people who took part in the authentic); and yet the appropriation of the improper, of that which does not belong, was in itself impossible, because every affirmation of the authentic had the effect of pushing the inauthentic to another place, where morality would once again raise its barriers. The conquest of the good thus necessarily implied a growth of the evil that had been repelled; every consolidation of the walls of paradise was matched by a deepening of the infernal abyss.

For us, who have been allotted not the slightest part of properness (or to whom, in the best of cases, only tiny fragments of the good have been imparted), there opens instead, perhaps for the first time, the possibility of an appropriation of impropriety as such, one that leaves no residue of Gehenna outside itself.

This is how one should understand the free-spirit and Gnostic doctrine of the impeccability of the perfect. This does not mean, as the crude falsifications of the polemicists and inquisitors would have it, that the perfect person can lay claim to committing the most repugnant crimes without sinning (this is rather the perverse fantasy of moralists of all ages); it means, on the contrary, that the perfect has appropriated all the possibilities of evil and impropriety and therefore cannot commit evil.

This, and nothing else, was the doctrinal content of the heresy that on November 12, 1210, sent the followers of Amalric of Bena to burn at the stake. Amalric interpreted the Apostle's claim that "God is all in all" as a radical theological development of the Platonic doctrine of the *chora*. God is in every thing as the place in which every thing is, or rather as the determination and the "topia" of every entity. The transcendent, therefore, is not a supreme entity above all things; rather, *the pure transcendent is the taking-place of every thing.*

God or the good or the place does not take place, but is the taking-place of the entities, their innermost exteriority. The being-worm of the worm, the being-stone of the stone, is divine. That the world is, that something can appear and have a face, that there is exteriority and non-latency as the determination and the limit of every thing: this is the good. Thus, precisely its being irreparably in the world is what transcends and exposes every worldly entity. Evil, on the other hand, is the reduction of the taking-place of things to a fact like others, the forgetting of the transcendence inherent in the very taking-place of things. With respect to these things, however, the good is not somewhere else; it is simply the point at which they grasp the taking-place proper to them, at which they touch their own non-transcendent matter.

In this sense—and only in this sense—the good must be defined as a self-grasping of evil, and salvation as the coming of the place to itself.

Principium indivuationis

WHATEVER IS the matheme of singularity, without which it is impossible to conceive either being or the individuation of singularity. How the Scholastics posed the problem of the *principium individuationis* is well known. Against Saint Thomas, who sought the place of individuation in matter, Duns Scotus conceived individuation as an addition to nature or common form (for example, humanity)—an addition not of another form or essence or property, but of an *ultima realitas*, of an "utmostness" of the form itself. Singularity adds nothing to the common form, if not a "haecceity" (as Etienne Gilson says: here we do not have individuation in virtue of the form, but individuation *of* the form). But for this reason, according to Duns Scotus, common form or nature must be indifferent to whatever singularity, must in itself be neither particular nor universal, neither one nor multiple, but such that it "does not scorn being posed with a whatever singular unity."

The limit of Duns Scotus is that he seems to conceive common nature as an anterior reality, which has the property of being indifferent to whatever singularity, and to which singularity adds only haecceity. Accordingly, he leaves unthought precisely that *quodlibet* that is inseparable from singularity and, without recognizing it, makes indifference the real root of individuation. But "quodlibetality" is not indifference; nor is it a predicate of singularity that expresses its dependence on common nature.

What then is the relationship between quodlibetality and indifference? How can we understand the indifference of the common human form with respect to singular humans? And what is the haecceity that constitutes the being of the singular?

We know that Guillaume de Champeaux, Peter Abelard's teacher, affirmed that "the idea is present in single individuals *non essentialiter, sed indifferenter.*" And Duns Scotus added that there is no difference of essence between common nature and haecceity. This means that the idea and common nature do not constitute the essence of singularity, that singularity is, in this sense, absolutely inessential, and that, consequently, the criterion of its difference should be sought elsewhere than in an essence or a concept. The relationship between the common and the singular can thus no longer be conceived as the persistence of an identical essence in single individuals, and therefore the very problem of individuation risks appearing as a pseudoproblem.

Nothing is more instructive in this regard than the way Spinoza conceives of the common. All bodies, he says, have it in common to express the divine attribute of extension (*Ethics*, Part II, Proposition 13, Lemma 2). And yet what is common cannot in any case constitute the essence of the single case (*Ethics*, Part II, Proposition 37). Decisive here is the idea of an *inessential* commonality, a solidarity that in no way concerns an essence. *Taking-place, the communication of singularities in the attribute of extension, does not unite them in essence, but scatters them in existence.*

Whatever is constituted not by the indifference of common nature with respect to singularities, but by the indifference of the common and the proper, of the genus and the species, of the essential and the accidental. Whatever is the thing *with all its properties*, none of which, however, constitutes difference. In-difference with respect to properties is what individuates and disseminates singularities, makes them lovable (quodlibetable). Just as the right human word is neither the appropriation of what is common (language) nor the communication of what is proper, so too the human face is neither the individuation of a generic *facies* nor the universalization of singular traits: It is whatever face, in which what belongs to common nature and what is proper are absolutely indifferent.

This is how we must read the theory of those medieval philosophers who held that the passage from potentiality to act, from common form to singularity, is not an event accomplished once and for all, but an infinite series of modal oscillations. The individuation of a singular existence is not a punctual fact, but a *linea generationis substantiae* that varies in every direction according to a continual gradation of growth and remission, of appropriation and impropriation. The image of the line is not gratuitous. In a line of writing the *ductus* of the hand passes continually from the common form of the letters to the particular marks that identify its singular presence, and no one, even using the scrupulous rigor of graphology, could ever trace the real division between these two spheres. So too in a face, human nature continually passes into existence, and it is precisely this incessant emergence that constitutes its expressivity. But it would be equally plausible to say the opposite: It is from the hundred idiosyncracies that characterize my way of writing the letter *p* or of pronouncing its phoneme that its common form is engendered. *Common and proper, genus and individual are only the two slopes dropping down from either side of the watershed of whatever.* As with Prince Myshkin in Dostoyevsky's *Idiot,* who can effortlessly imitate anyone's handwriting and sign any signature ("the humble Pafnutius signed here"), the particular and the generic become indifferent, and precisely this is the "idiocy," in other words, the particularity of the whatever. The passage from potentiality to act, from language to the word, from the common to the proper, comes about every time as a shuttling in both directions along a line of sparkling alternation on which common nature and singularity, potentiality and act change roles and interpenetrate. The being that is engendered on this line is whatever being, and the manner in which it passes from the common to the proper and from the proper to the common is called usage—or rather, *ethos.*

VI

Ease

ACCORDING TO the Talmud, two places are reserved for each person, one in Eden and the other in Gehenna. The just person, after being found innocent, receives a place in Eden plus that of a neighbor who was damned. The unjust person, after being judged guilty, receives a place in hell plus that of a neighbor who was saved. Thus the Bible says of the just, "In their land they receive double," and of the unjust, "Destroy them with a double destruction."

In the topology of this Haggadah of the Talmud, the essential element is not so much the cartographic distinction between Eden and Gehenna, but rather the adjacent place that each person inevitably receives. At the point when one reaches one's final state and fulfills one's own destiny, one finds oneself for that very reason in the place of the neighbor. What is most proper to every creature is thus its substitutability, its being in any case in the place of the other.

Toward the end of his life the great Arabist Louis Massignon, who in his youth had daringly converted to Catholicism in the land of Islam, founded a community called Badaliya, a name deriving from the Arabic term for "substitution." The members took a vow to live *substituting themselves* for someone else, that is, to be Christians *in the place of others*.

This substitution can be understood in two ways. The first conceives of the fall or sin of the other only as the opportunity for one's own salvation: A loss is compensated for by an election, a fall by an ascent, according to an economy of compensation that is hardly edifying. (In this sense, Badaliya would be nothing but a belated ransom paid for Massignon's homosexual friend who committed suicide in prison in Valencia in 1921, and from whom he had had to distance himself at the time of his conversion.)

But there is also another interpretation of Badaliya. According to Massignon, in fact, substituting oneself for another does not mean compensating for what the other lacks, nor correcting his or her errors, but *exiling oneself to the other as he or she is* in order to offer Christ hospitality in the other's own soul, in the other's own taking-place. This substitution no longer knows a place of its own, but the taking-place of every single being is always already common—an empty space offered to the one, irrevocable hospitality.

The destruction of the wall dividing Eden from Gehenna is thus the secret intention that animates Badaliya. In this community there is no place that is not vicarious, and Eden and Gehenna are only the names of this reciprocal substitution. Against the hypocritical fiction of the unsubstitutability of the individual, which in our culture serves only to guarantee its universal representability, Badaliya presents an unconditioned substitutability, without either representation or possible description—an absolutely unrepresentable community.

In this way, the multiple common place, which the Talmud presents as the place of the neighbor that each person inevitably receives, is nothing but the coming to itself of each singularity, its being whatever—in other words, such as it is.

Ease is the proper name of this unrepresentable space. The term "ease" in fact designates, according to its etymology, the space adjacent (*ad-jacens, adjacentia*), the empty place where each can move freely, in a semantic constellation where spatial proximity borders on opportune time (*ad-agio*, moving at ease) and convenience borders on the correct relation. The Provençal poets (whose songs first introduce the term into Romance languages in the form *aizi, aizimen*) make ease a *terminus technicus* in their poetics, designating the very place of love. Or better, it designates not so much the place of love, but rather love as the experience of taking-place in a whatever singularity. In this sense, ease names perfectly that "free use of the proper" that, according to an expression of Friedrich Hölderlin's, is "the most difficult task." "*Mout mi semblatz de bel aizin.*" This is the greeting that, in Jaufré Rudel's song, the lovers exchange when they meet.

V I I

Maneries

MEDIEVAL LOGIC has a term whose exact etymology and proper meaning still elude the patient study of historians. One source, in effect, attributes to Jean Roscelin and his followers the claim that genera and universals are *maneries*. John of Salisbury, who cites the term in his *Metalogicus*, saying that he does not understand it fully (*incertum habeo*), seems to derive its etymology from *manere*, to persist ("one calls manner the number and the state of things in which each thing persists as it is"). What could these authors have had in mind when they spoke of being at its most universal as a "manner"? Or rather, why did they introduce this third figure beside genus and species?

Uguccione da Pisa's definition suggests that what these authors call "manner" is neither generic nor particular, but something like an exemplary singularity or a multiple singularity. "Species is called manner," he writes, "as when one says: grass of this species, that is, manner, grows in my garden." The logicians speak in such cases of an "intellectual indication" (*demonstratio ad intellectum*), insofar as "one thing is shown and another thing is meant." Manner, then, is neither generic nor individual: It is an exemplar, in other words a whatever singularity. It is probable, then, that the term *maneries* derives neither from *manere* (to express the dwelling place of being in itself, Plotinus's *monè*, or the *manentia* or *mansio* of the medieval philosophers) nor from *manus* or hand (as the modern philologists would have it), but rather from *manare*, and thus it refers to being in its rising forth. This is not, in terms of the division that dominates Western ontology, either an essence or an existence, but a *manner of rising forth*; not a being that is *in* this or that mode, but a being that is *its* mode of being, and thus, while remaining singular and not indifferent, is multiple and valid for all.

Only the idea of this modality of rising forth, this original mannerism of being, allows us to find a common passage between ontology and ethics. The being that does not remain below itself, that does not *presuppose* itself as a hidden essence that chance or destiny would then condemn to the torment of qualifications, but rather *exposes* itself in its qualifications, *is* its *thus* without remainder—such a being is neither accidental nor necessary, but is, so to speak, *continually engendered from its own manner*.

Plotinus had to have this kind of being in mind when, trying to define the freedom and the will of the one, he explained that we cannot say that "it happened to be thus," but only that it "is as it is, without being master of its own being" and that "it does not remain below itself, but makes use of itself as it is" and that it is not thus by necessity, in the sense that it could not be otherwise, but because "*thus* is best."

Perhaps the only way to understand this free *use of the*

self, a way that does not, however, treat existence as a property, is to think of it as a *habitus*, an *ethos*. Being engendered from one's own manner of being is, in effect, the very definition of habit (this is why the Greeks spoke of a second nature): *That manner is ethical that does not befall us and does not found us but engenders us.* And this being engendered from one's own manner is the only happiness really possible for humans.

But a manner of rising forth is also the place of whatever singularity, its *principium individuationis*. For the being that is its own manner this is not, in effect, so much a property that determines and identifies it as an essence, but rather an improperty; what makes it exemplary, however, is that this improperty is assumed and appropriated as its unique being. The example is only the being of that of which it is the example; but this being does not belong to it, it is perfectly common. The improperty, which we expose as our proper being, manner, which we *use*, engenders us. It is our second, happier, nature.

VIII

Demonic

THE TENACITY of the recurrent heretical tendency that demands the ultimate salvation of Satan is well known. The curtain rises on Robert Walser's world when the very last demon of Gehenna has been escorted back to heaven, when the process of the history of salvation has been completed, leaving no residue.

It is astounding that this century's two most lucid observers of the incomparable horror that surrounded them—Kafka and Walser—both present us with a world from which evil in its traditional supreme expression, the demonic, has disappeared. Neither Klamm nor the Count nor Kafka's clerks and judges, nor even less Walser's creatures, despite their ambiguity, would ever figure in a demonological catalogue. If something like a demonic element survives in the world of these two authors, it is rather in the form Spinoza may have had in mind when he wrote that the devil is only the weakest of creatures and the most distant from God; as such—that is, insofar as the devil is essentially impotent—not only can it not do us harm, but on the contrary it is what most needs our help and our prayers. It is, in every being that exists, the possibility of not-being that silently calls for our help (or, if you wish, the devil is nothing other than divine impotence or the power of not-being in God). Evil is only our inadequate reaction when faced with this demonic element, our fearful retreat from it in order to exercise—founding ourselves in this flight—some power of being. Impotence or the power to not-be is the root of evil only in this secondary sense. Fleeing from our own impotence, or rather trying to adopt it as a weapon, we construct the malevolent power that oppresses those who show us their weakness; and failing our innermost possibility of not-being, we fall away from the only thing that makes love possible. Creation—or existence—is not the victorious struggle of a power to be against a power to not-be; it is rather the impotence of God with respect to his own impotence, his allowing—being able to *not* not-be—a contingency to be. Or rather: It is the birth in God of love.

This is why it is not so much the natural innocence of creatures that Kafka and Walser allow to prevail against divine omnipotence as the natural innocence of temptation. Their demon is not a tempter, but a being infinitely susceptible to being tempted. Eichmann, an absolutely banal man who was tempted to evil precisely by the powers of right and law, is the terrible confirmation through which our era has revenged itself on their diagnosis.

I X

Bartleby

KANT DEFINES the schema of possibility as "the determination of the representation of a thing in whatever time." It seems that the form of the *whatever*, an irreducible *quodlibet*-like character, inheres in potentiality and possibility, insofar as they are distinct from reality. But what potentiality are we dealing with here? And what does "whatever" mean in this context?

Of the two modes in which, according to Aristotle, every potentiality is articulated, the decisive one is that which the philosopher calls "the potentiality to not-be" (*dynamis me einai*) or also impotence (*adynamia*). For if it is true that whatever being always has a potential character, it is equally certain that it is not capable of only this or that specific act, nor is it therefore simply incapable, lacking in power, nor even less is it indifferently capable of everything, all-powerful: The being that is properly whatever is able to not-be; it is capable of its own impotence.

Everything rests here on the mode in which the passage from potentiality to act comes about. The symmetry between the potentiality to be and the potentiality to not-be is, in effect, only apparent. In the potentiality to be, potentiality has as its object a certain act, in the sense that for it *energhein*, being-in-act, can only mean passing to a determinate activity (this is why Schelling defines the potentiality that cannot not pass into action as *blind*); as for the potentiality to not-be, on the other hand, the act can never consist of a simple transition *de potentia ad actum:* It is, in other words, a potentiality that has as its object potentiality itself, a *potentia potentiae*.

Only a power that is capable of both power and impotence, then, is the supreme power. If every power is equally the power to be and the power to not-be, the passage to action can only come about by transporting (Aristotle says "saving") in the act its own power to not-be. This means that, even though every pianist necessarily has the potential to play and the potential to not-play, Glenn Gould is, however, the only one who can *not* not-play, and, directing his potentiality not only to the act but to his own impotence, he plays, so to speak, with his potential to not-play. While his ability simply negates and abandons his potential to not-play, his mastery conserves and exercises in the act not his potential to play (this is the position of irony that affirms the superiority of the positive potentiality over the act), but rather his potential to not-play.

In *De anima* Aristotle articulates this theory in absolute terms with respect to the supreme theme of metaphysics. If thought were in fact only the potentiality to think this or that intelligibility, he argues, it would always already have passed through to the act and it would remain necessarily inferior to its own object. But thought, in its essence, is pure potentiality; in other words, it is also the potentiality to not think, and, as such, as possible or material intellect, Aristotle compares it to a writing tablet on which nothing is written. (This is the celebrated image that the Latin translators render with the expression *tabula rasa*, even if, as the ancient commentators noted, one should speak rather of a *rasum tabulae*, that is, of the layer of wax covering the tablet that the stylus engraves.)

Thanks to this potentiality to not-think, thought can turn back to itself (to its pure potentiality) and be, at its apex, the thought of thought. What it thinks here, however, is not an object, a being-in-act, but that layer of wax, that *rasum tabulae* that is nothing but its own passivity, its own pure potentiality (to not-think): In the potentiality that thinks itself, action and passion coincide and the writing tablet writes by itself or, rather, writes its own passivity.

The perfect act of writing comes not from a power to write, but from an impotence that turns back on itself and in this way comes to itself as a pure act (which Aristotle calls agent intellect). This is why in the Arab tradition agent intellect has the form of an angel whose name is *Qalam*, Pen, and its place is an unfathomable potentiality. Bartleby, a scribe who does not simply cease writing but "prefers not to," is the extreme image of this angel that writes nothing but its potentiality to not-write.

x   .

Irreparable

QUESTIO 91 of the supplement to Saint Thomas's *Summa Theologica* is titled *De qualitate mundi post iudicium.* This section investigates the condition of nature after the universal judgment: Will there be a *renovatio* of the universe? Will the movement of celestial bodies cease? Will the splendor of the elements increase? What will happen to the animals and plants? The logical difficulty that these questions run up against is that, if the sensible world was ordered to fit the dignity and the habitation of imperfect humans, then what sense can that world have when those humans arrive at their supernatural destination? How can nature survive the accomplishment of its final cause? To these questions Robert Walser's promenade on the "good and faithful earth" admits only one response: The "wonderful fields," the "grass wet with dew," the "gentle roar of the water," the "recreational club decorated with bright banners," the girls, the hairdresser's salon, Mrs. Wilke's room, all will be just as it is, irreparably, but precisely this will be its novelty. The Irreparable is the monogram that Walser's writing engraves into things. Irreparable means that these things are consigned without remedy to their being-thus, that they are precisely and only their *thus* (nothing is more foreign to Walser than the pretense of being other than what one is); but irreparable also means that for them there is literally no shelter possible, that in their being-thus they are absolutely exposed, absolutely abandoned.

This implies that both necessity and contingency, those two crosses of Western thought, have disappeared from the *post iudicium* world. The world is now and forever necessarily contingent or contingently necessary. Between the *not being able to not-be* that sanctions the decree of necessity and the *being able to not-be* that defines fluctuating contingency, the finite world suggests a contingency to the second power that does not found any freedom: It *is capable of not not-being,* it is capable of the irreparable.

This is why the ancient dictum that says, "If nature could speak it would lament" makes no sense here. After the judgment, animals, plants, things, all the elements and creatures of the world, having completed their theological task, would then enjoy an incorruptible fallenness—above them floats something like a profane halo. Therefore nothing could define the statute of the coming singularity better than these lines that close one of the late poems of Hölderlin-Scardanelli:

> *(It) appears with a day of gold*
> *and the fulfillment is without lament.*

xi

Ethics

THE FACT that must constitute the point of departure for any discourse on ethics is that there is no essence, no historical or spiritual vocation, no biological destiny that humans must enact or realize. This is the only reason why something like an ethics can exist, because it is clear that if humans were or had to be this or that substance, this or that destiny, no ethical experience would be possible — there would be only tasks to be done.

This does not mean, however, that humans are not, and do not have to be, something, that they are simply consigned to nothingness and therefore can freely decide whether to be or not to be, to adopt or not to adopt this or that destiny (nihilism and decisionism coincide at this point). There is in effect something that humans are and have to be, but this something is not an essence nor properly a thing: *It is the simple fact of one's own existence as possibility or potentiality*. But precisely because of this things become complicated; precisely because of this ethics becomes effective.

Since the being most proper to humankind is being one's own possibility or potentiality, then and only for this reason (that is, insofar as humankind's most proper being — being potential — is in a certain sense lacking, insofar as it can not-be, it is therefore devoid of foundation and humankind is not always already in possession of it), humans have and feel a debt. Humans, in their potentiality to be and to not-be, are, in other words, always already in debt; they always already have a bad conscience without having to commit any blameworthy act.

This is all that is meant by the old theological doctrine of original sin. Morality, on the other hand, refers this doctrine to a blameworthy act humans have committed and, in this way, shackles their potentiality, turning it back toward the past. The recognition of evil is older and more original than any blameworthy act, and it rests solely on the fact that, being and having to be only its possibility or potentiality, humankind fails itself in a certain sense and has to appropriate this failing—it has to *exist* as *potentiality*. Like Perceval in the novel by Chrétien de Troyes, humans are guilty for what they lack, for an act they have not committed.

This is why ethics has no room for repentance; this is why the only ethical experience (which, as such, cannot be a task or a subjective decision) is the experience of being (one's own) potentiality, of being (one's own) possibility—exposing, that is, in every form one's own amorphousness and in every act one's own inactuality.

The only evil consists instead in the decision to remain in a deficit of existence, to appropriate the power to not-be as a substance and a foundation beyond existence; or rather (and this is the destiny of morality), to regard potentiality itself, which is the most proper mode of human existence. as a fault that must always be repressed.

x i i

Dim Stockings

IN THE early 1970s there was an advertisement shown in Paris movie theaters that promoted a well-known brand of French stockings, "Dim" stockings. It showed a group of young women dancing together. Anyone who watched even a few of its images, however distractedly, would have a hard time forgetting the special impression of synchrony and dissonance, of confusion and singularity, of communication and estrangement that emanated from the bodies of the smiling dancers. This impression relied on a trick: Each dancer was filmed separately and later the single pieces were brought together over a single sound track. But that facile trick, that calculated asymmetry of the movement of long legs sheathed in the same inexpensive commodity, that slight disjunction between the gestures, wafted over the audience a promise of happiness unequivocally related to the human body.

In the 1920s when the process of capitalist commodification began to invest the human body, observers who were by no means favorable to the phenomenon could not help but notice a positive aspect to it, as if they were confronted with the corrupt text of a prophecy that went beyond the limits of the capitalist mode of production and were faced with the task of deciphering it. This is what gave rise to Siegfried Kracauer's observations on the "girls" and Walter Benjamin's reflections on the decay of the aura.

The commodification of the human body, while subjecting it to the iron laws of massification and exchange value, seemed at the same time to redeem the body from the stigma of ineffability that had marked it for millennia. Breaking away from the double chains of biological destiny and individual biography, it took its leave of both the inarticulate cry of the tragic body and the dumb silence of the comic body, and thus appeared for the first time perfectly communicable, entirely illuminated. The epochal process of the emancipation of the human body from its theological foundations was thus accomplished in the dances of the "girls," in the advertising images, and in the gait of fashion models. This process had already been imposed at an industrial level when, at the beginning of the nineteenth century, the invention of lithography and photography encouraged the inexpensive distribution of pornographic images: Neither generic nor individual, neither an image of the divinity nor an animal form, the body now became something truly *whatever*.

Here the commodity betrays its secret solidarity (glimpsed by Marx) with the theological antinomies. The phrase in Genesis "in the image and likeness" rooted the human figure in God, bound it in this way to an invisible archetype, and founded with it the paradoxical concept of an absolutely immaterial resemblance. While commodification unanchors the body from its theological model, it still preserves the resemblance: *Whatever is a resemblance without archetype—in other words, an Idea*. Hence, even though the perfectly fungible beauty of the technologized body no longer has anything to do with the appearance of a *unicum* that troubled the old Trojan princes when they saw Helen at the Skaian gates, there is still in both of them something like a resemblance ("seeing her terribly resemble the immortal goddesses"). This is also the basis of the exodus of the human figure from the artwork of our times and the decline of portraiture: The task of the portrait is grasping a unicity, but to grasp a whateverness one needs a photographic lens.

In a certain sense, the process of emancipation is as old as the invention of the arts. From the instant that a hand drew or sculpted the human figure for the first time, Pygmalion's dream was already there to guide it: to form not simply an image of the loved body, but another body in that image, shattering the organic barrier that obstructs the uncondi-tioned human claim to happiness.

Today, in the age of the complete domination of the com-modity form over all aspects of social life, what remains of the subdued, senseless promise of happiness that we received in the darkness of movie theaters from dancers sheathed in Dim stockings? Never has the human body—above all the female body—been so massively manipulated as today and, so to speak, imagined from top to bottom by the techniques of adver-tising and commodity production: The opacity of sexual differences has been belied by the transsexual body; the incommunicable foreignness of the singular *physis* has been abolished by its mediatization as spectacle; the mortality of the organic body has been put in question by its traffic with the body without organs of commodities; the intimacy of erotic life has been refuted by pornography. And yet the process of technologization, instead of materially investing the body, was aimed at the construction of a separate sphere that had practically no point of contact with it: What was technologized was not the body, but its image. Thus the glorious body of advertising has become the mask behind which the fragile, slight human body continues its precarious existence, and the geometrical splendor of the "girls" covers over the long lines of the naked, anonymous bodies led to their death in the *Lagers* (camps), or the thousands of corpses mangled in the daily slaughter on the highways.

To appropriate the historic transformations of human nature that capitalism wants to limit to the spectacle, to link together image and body in a space where they can no longer be separated, and thus to forge the whatever body, whose *physis* is resemblance — this is the good that humanity must learn how to wrest from commodities in their decline. Advertising and pornography, which escort the commodity to the grave like hired mourners, are the unknowing midwives of this new body of humanity.

xiii

Halos

THERE IS a well-known parable about the Kingdom of the Messiah that Walter Benjamin (who heard it from Gershom Scholem) recounted one evening to Ernst Bloch, who in turn transcribed it in *Spuren:* "A rabbi, a real cabalist, once said that in order to establish the reign of peace it is not necessary to destroy everything nor to begin a completely new world. It is sufficient to displace this cup or this bush or this stone just a little, and thus everything. But this small displacement is so difficult to achieve and its measure is so difficult to find that, with regard to the world, humans are incapable of it and it is necessary that the Messiah come." Benjamin's version of the story goes like this: "The *Hassidim* tell a story about the world to come that says everything there will be just as it is here. Just as our room is now, so it will be in the world to come; where our baby sleeps now, there too it will sleep in the other world. And the clothes we wear in this world, those too we will wear there. Everything will be as it is now, just a little different."

There is nothing new about the thesis that the Absolute is identical to this world. It was stated in its extreme form by Indian logicians with the axiom, "Between Nirvana and the world there is not the slightest difference." What is new, instead, is the tiny displacement that the story introduces in the messianic world. And yet it is precisely this tiny displacement, this "everything will be as it is now, just a little different," that is difficult to explain. This cannot refer simply to real circumstances, in the sense that the nose of the blessed one will become a little shorter, or that the cup on the table will be displaced exactly one-half centimeter, or that the dog outside will stop barking. The tiny displacement does not refer to the state of things, but to their sense and their limits. It does not take place in things, but at their periphery, in the space of ease between every thing and itself. This means that even though perfection does not imply a real mutation it does not simply involve an external state of things, an incurable "so be it." On the contrary, the parable introduces a possibility there where everything is perfect, an "otherwise" where everything is finished forever, and precisely this is its irreducible aporia. But how is it possible that things be "otherwise" once everything is definitively finished?

The theory developed by Saint Thomas in his short treatise on halos is instructive in this regard. The beatitude of the chosen, he argues, includes all the goods that are necessary for the perfect workings of human nature, and therefore nothing essential can be added. There is, however, something that can be added in surplus (*superaddi*), an "accidental reward that is added to the essential," that is not necessary for beatitude and does not alter it substantially, but that simply makes it more brilliant (*clarior*).

The halo is this supplement added to perfection — something like the vibration of that which is perfect, the glow at its edges.

Saint Thomas does not seem to be aware of the audacity of introducing an accidental element into the *status perfectionis*, and this by itself would be enough to explain why the *questio* on halos remains practically without commentary in the Latin Patristics. The halo is not a *quid*, a property or an essence that is added to beatitude: It is an absolutely inessential supplement. But it is precisely for this reason that Saint Thomas so unexpectedly anticipates the theory that several years later Duns Scotus would pose as a challenge on the problem of individuation. In response to the question of whether one of the blessed can merit a halo brighter than the halos of others, he said (against the theory whereby what is finished can neither grow nor diminish) that beatitude does not arrive at perfection singularly but as a species, "just as fire, as a species, is the most subtle of bodies; nothing, therefore, prevents one halo from being brighter than another just as one fire can be more subtle than another."

The halo is thus the individuation of a beatitude, the becoming singular of that which is perfect. As in Duns Scotus, this individuation does not imply the addition of a new essence or a change in its nature, but rather its singular completion; unlike Scotus, however, for Saint

Thomas the singularity here is not a final determination of being, but an unraveling or an indetermination of its limits: a paradoxical *individuation by indetermination*.

One can think of the halo, in this sense, as a zone in which possibility and reality, potentiality and actuality, become indistinguishable. The being that has reached its end, that has consumed all of its possibilities, thus receives as a gift a supplemental possibility. This is that *potentia permixta actui* (or that *actus permixtus potentiae*) that a brilliant fourteenth-century philosopher called *actus confusionis*, a fusional act, insofar as specific form or nature is not preserved in it, but mixed and dissolved in a new birth with no residue. This imperceptible trembling of the finite that makes its limits indeterminate and allows it to blend, to make itself whatever, is the tiny displacement that every thing must accomplish in the messianic world. Its beatitude is that of a potentiality that comes only after the act, of matter that does not remain beneath the form, but surrounds it with a halo.

XIV

Pseudonym

EVERY LAMENT is always a lament for language, just as all praise is principally praise of the name. These are the extremes that define the domain and the scope of human language, its way of referring to things. Lament arises when nature feels betrayed by meaning; when the name perfectly says the thing, language culminates in the song of praise, in the sanctification of the name. Robert Walser's language seems to ignore them both. Ontotheological pathos—both in the form of unsayability and in the (equivalent) form of absolute sayability—always remained foreign to his writing, which maintained a delicate balance between "modest imprecision" and a mannerist stereotype. (Here too, Scardanelli's protocol-laden language is the herald that announces the prose pieces of Berne or Waldau a century early.)

If in the West language has constantly been used as a machine to bring into being the name of God and to found in the name its own power of reference, then Walser's language has outlived its theological task. A nature that has exhausted its destiny among created beings is matched by a language that has declined any pretense of denomination. The semantic status of his prose coincides with that of the pseudonym or the nickname. It is as if every word were preceded by an invisible "so-called," "pseudo-," and "would-be" or followed (as in the late inscriptions where the appearance of the agnomen marked the passage from the trinomial Latin system to the uninomial medieval system) by a *"qui et vocatur...,"* almost as if every term raised an objection against its own denominative power. Like the little dancers to which Walser compares his prose pieces, the words "dead tired" decline any pretense of rigor. If any grammatical form corresponds to this exhausted state of language it is the supine, that is, a word that has completely achieved its "declension" in cases and moods and is now "stretched out on its back," exposed and neutral.

The petty bourgeois distrust of language is transformed here into a modesty of language with respect to its referent. This referent is no longer nature betrayed by meaning, nor its transfiguration in the name, but it is what is held—unuttered—in the pseudonym or in the ease between the name and the nickname. In a letter to Max Rychner, Walser speaks of this "fascination of not uttering something absolutely." "Figure"—that is, precisely the term that expresses in Saint Paul's epistles what passes away in the face of the nature that does not die—is the name Walser gives to the life that is born in this gap.

xv

Without Classes

IF WE had once again to conceive of the fortunes of humanity in terms of class, then today we would have to say that there are no longer social classes, but just a single planetary petty bourgeoisie, in which all the old social classes are dissolved: The petty bourgeoisie has inherited the world and is the form in which humanity has survived nihilism.

But this is also exactly what fascism and Nazism understood, and to have clearly seen the irrevocable decline of the old social subjects constitutes their insuperable cachet of modernity. (From a strictly political point of view fascism and Nazism have not been overcome, and we still live under their sign.) They represented, however, a national petty bourgeoisie still attached to a false popular identity in which dreams of bourgeois grandeur were an active force. The planetary petty bourgeoisie has instead freed itself from these dreams and has taken over the aptitude of the proletariat to refuse any recognizable social identity. The petty bourgeois nullify all that exists with the same gesture in which they seem obstinately to adhere to it: They know only the improper and the inauthentic and even refuse the idea of a discourse that could be proper to them. That which constituted the truth and falsity of the peoples and generations that have followed one another on the earth—differences of language, of dialect, of ways of life, of character, of custom, and even the physical particularities of each person—has lost any meaning for them and any capacity for expression and communication. In the petty bourgeoisie, the diversities that have marked the tragicomedy of universal history are brought together and exposed in a phantasmagorical vacuousness.

But the absurdity of individual existence, inherited from the subbase of nihilism, has become in the meantime so senseless that it has lost all pathos and been transformed, brought out into the open, into an everyday exhibition: Nothing resembles the life of this new humanity more than advertising footage from which every trace of the advertised product has been wiped out. The contradiction of the petty bourgeois, however, is that they still search in the footage for the product they were cheated of, obstinately trying, against all odds, to make their own an identity that has become in reality absolutely improper and insignificant to them. Shame and arrogance, conformity and marginality remain thus the poles of all their emotional registers.

The fact is that the senselessness of their existence runs up against a final absurdity, against which all advertising runs aground: death itself. In death the petty bourgeois confront the ultimate expropriation, the ultimate frustration of individuality: life in all its nakedness, the pure incommunicable, where their shame can finally rest in peace. Thus they use death to cover the secret that they must resign themselves to acknowledging: that even life in its nakedness is, in truth, improper and purely exterior to them, that for them there is no shelter on earth.

This means that the planetary petty bourgeoisie is probably the form in which humanity is moving toward its own destruction. But this also means that the petty bourgeoisie represents an opportunity unheard of in the history of humanity that it must at all costs not let slip away. Because if instead of continuing to search for a proper identity in the already improper and senseless form of individuality, humans were to succeed in belonging to this impropriety as such, in making of the proper being-thus not an identity and an individual property but a singularity without identity, a common and absolutely exposed singularity—if humans could, that is, not be-thus in this or that particular biography, but be only *the* thus, their singular exteriority and their face, then they would for the first time enter into a community without presuppositions and without subjects, into a communication without the incommunicable.

Selecting in the new planetary humanity those characteristics that allow for its survival, removing the thin diaphragm that separates bad mediatized advertising from the perfect exteriority that communicates only itself—this is the political task of our generation.

individuality & identity not as good as Singularity

identity having as a border limits

Potential having as a border
thresholds

identity ≃ singularity attached to an
empty space

XVI

Outside

[handwritten notes: "Identity" and "Potential (Whatever) singularity w/out identity"]

WHATEVER IS the figure of pure singularity. Whatever singularity has no identity, it is not determinate with respect to a concept, but neither is it simply indeterminate; rather it is determined only through its relation to an *idea*, that is, to the totality of its possibilities. Through this relation, as Kant said, singularity borders all possibility and thus receives its *omnimoda determinatio* not from its participation in a determinate concept or some actual property (being red, Italian, Communist), but *only by means of this bordering*. It belongs to a whole, but without this belonging's being able to be represented by a real condition: Belonging, being-*such*, is here only the relation to an empty and indeterminate totality.

In Kantian terms this means that what is in question in this bordering is not a limit (*Schranke*) that knows no exteriority, but a threshold (*Grenze*), that is, a point of contact with an external space that must remain empty.

Whatever adds to singularity only an emptiness, only a threshold: Whatever is a singularity plus an empty space, a singularity that is *finite* and, nonetheless, indeterminable according to a concept. But a singularity plus an empty space can only be a pure exteriority, a pure exposure. *Whatever, in this sense, is the event of an outside.* What is thought in the architranscendental *quodlibet* is, therefore, what is most difficult to think: the absolutely non-thing experience of a pure exteriority.

It is important here that the notion of the "outside" is expressed in many European languages by a word that means "at the door" (*fores* in Latin is the door of the house, *thyrathen* in Greek literally means "at the threshold"). The *outside* is not another space that resides beyond a determinate space, but rather, it is the passage, the exteriority that gives it access—in a word, it is its face, its *eidos*.

The threshold is not, in this sense, another thing with respect to the limit; it is, so to speak, the experience of the limit itself, the experience of being-*within* an *outside*. This *ek-stasis* is the gift that singularity gathers from the empty hands of humanity.

xvii

Homonyms

IN JUNE 1902, a thirty-year-old English logician wrote Gottlob Frege a short letter in which he claimed to have discovered in one of the postulates of *The Basic Laws of Arithmetic* an antinomy that threatened to call into question the very foundations of the "paradise" that Cantor's set theory had created for mathematicians.

With his usual acumen, but not without some distress, Frege quickly understood what was at stake in the young Bertrand Russell's letter: nothing less than the possibility of passing from a concept to its extension, that is, the very possibility of thinking in terms of classes. "When we say that certain objects all have a certain property," Russell explained later, "we suppose that this property is a definite object, that it can be distinct from the objects that belong to it; we further suppose that the objects that have the property in question form a class, and that this class is, in some way, a new entity distinct from each of its elements." Precisely these unstated, obvious presuppositions were brought into question by the paradox of the "class of all the classes that are not members of themselves," which today has become an amusement for cocktail parties, but was clearly serious enough to be a long-term stumbling block to Frege's intellectual production and to force its discoverer to spend years marshaling every suitable means to limit its consequences. Despite David Hilbert's insistent warning, the logicians were driven out of their paradise once and for all.

As Frege guessed, and as we begin perhaps to see more clearly today, underlying these paradoxes of set theory is the same problem that Kant, in his letter to Marcus Herz of February 21, 1772, formulated in the question: "How do our representations refer to objects?" What does it mean to say that the concept "red" designates red objects? And is it true that every concept determines a class that constitutes its extension? What Russell's paradox brought to light was the existence of properties or concepts (which he called non-predicative) that do not determine a class (or rather that cannot determine a class without producing antinomies). Russell linked these properties (and the pseudoclasses that derive from them) with those in whose definition appear the "apparent variables" constituted by the terms "all," "every," and "any."[2] The classes that arise from these expressions are "illegitimate totalities," which pretend to be part of the totality they define (something like a concept that demands to be part of its own extension). Against these classes, the logicians (unaware that their warnings unfailingly contain these variables) issue more and more prohibitions and plant their border markers: "Anything that implies all the members of a class must not itself be one of them"; "all that in any way concerns every or each member of a class must not be a member of that class"; "if any expression contains an apparent variable, it must not be one of the possible values of that variable."

Unfortunately for logicians, non-predicative expressions are much more numerous than one might think. Actually, since every term refers by definition to every and any member of its extension, and can, furthermore, refer to itself, one can say that all (or almost all) words can be presented as classes that, according to the formulation of the paradox, both are and are not members themselves.

It is not worth objecting against this that one never mistakes the term "shoe" for a shoe. Here an insufficient conception of self-reference blocks us from grasping the crux of the problem: What is in question is not the word "shoe" in its acoustic or graphic form (the *suppositio materialis* of medieval logicians), but the word "shoe" precisely in its signifying the shoe (or, *a parte objecti*, the shoe in its being signified by the term "shoe"). Even if we can completely distinguish a shoe from the term "shoe," it is still much more difficult to distinguish a shoe from its being-called-(shoe), from its *being-in-language*. Being-called or being-in-language is the non-predicative property par excellence that belongs to each member of a class and at the same time makes its belonging an aporia. This is also the content of the paradox that Frege once stated in writing, "The concept 'horse' is not a concept" (and that Milner, in a recent book, expressed as, "The linguistic term has no proper name"). In other words, if we try to grasp a concept as such, it is fatally transformed into an object, and the price we pay is no longer being able to distinguish it from the conceived thing.

This aporia of intentionality, whereby it cannot be intended without becoming an *intentum*, was familiar to medieval logicians as the paradox of "cognitive being." According to the formulation of Meister Eckhart, "If the form (*species*) or image by which a thing is seen and known were other than the thing itself, we would never be able to know the thing either through it or in it. But if the form or image were completely indistinct from the thing, it would be useless for knowledge. . . . If the form that is in the soul had the nature of an object, then we would not know through it the thing of which it is the form, because if it itself were an object it would lead us to the knowledge of itself and it would divert us from the knowledge of the thing." (In other words, in the terms that interest us here, if the word through which a thing is expressed were either something other than the thing itself or identical to it, then it would not be able to express the thing.)

Not a hierarchy of types (like the one proposed by Russell that so irritated the young Wittgenstein), but only a theory of ideas is in a position to disentangle thought from the aporias of linguistic being (or better, to transform them into euporias). Aristotle expressed this with unsurpassable clarity when he characterized the relationship between the

Platonic idea and multiple phenomena. This passage is deprived of its real meaning in the modern editions of the *Metaphysics*, but in the more authoritative manuscript it reads: "According to their participation, the plurality of synonyms is homonymous with respect to ideas" (*Metaphysics* 987b10).

Synonyms for Aristotle are entities that have the same name and the same definition: in other words, phenomena insofar as they are members of a coherent class, that is, insofar as they belong to a set through participation in a common concept. These same phenomena, however, that relate to each other as synonyms become homonyms if considered with respect to the idea (homonyms, according to Aristotle, are objects that have the same names but different definitions). Thus the single horses are synonyms with respect to the concept horse, but homonyms with respect to the idea of the horse—just as in Russell's paradox the same object both belongs and does not belong to a class.

But what is the idea that constitutes the homonymy of multiple synonyms and that, persisting in every class, withdraws its members from their predicative belonging to make them simple homonyms, to show their pure dwelling in language? That with respect to which the synonym is homonymous is neither an object nor a concept, but is instead its own having-name, its own belonging, or rather its being-in-language. This can neither be named in turn nor shown, but only grasped through an anaphoric movement. Hence the principle—which is decisive even if it is rarely thematized as such—according to which the idea does not have a proper name, but is only expressed by means of the anaphora *autò:* the idea of a thing is the thing *itself.* This anonymous homonymy is the idea.

But for this very reason it constitutes the homonym as whatever. *Whatever is singularity insofar as it relates not (only) to the concept, but (also) to the idea.* This relation does not found a new class, but is, in each class, that which draws singularity from its synonymy, from its belonging to a class, not toward any absence of name or belonging, but toward the name *itself,* toward a pure and anonymous homonymy. While the network of concepts continually introduces synonymous relations, the idea is that which intervenes every time to shatter the pretense of absoluteness in these relations, showing their inconsistency. *Whatever* does not therefore mean only (in the words of Alain Badiou) "subtracted from the authority of language, without any possible denomination, indiscernible"; it means more exactly that which, holding itself in simple homonymy, in pure being-called, is precisely and only for this reason unnameable: the being-in-language of the non-linguistic.

What remains without name here is the being-named, the name itself (*nomen innominabile*); only being-in-language is subtracted from the authority of language. According to a Platonic tautology, which we are still far from understanding, the idea of a thing is the thing itself; *the name, insofar as it names a thing, is nothing but the thing insofar as it is named by the name.*

xviii

Shekinah

WHEN GUY Debord published *Society of the Spectacle* in November 1967, the transformation of politics and of all social life into a spectacular phantasmagoria had not yet reached the extreme form that today has become perfectly familiar. This fact makes the implacable lucidity of his diagnosis all the more remarkable.

Capitalism in its final form, he argued—radicalizing the Marxian analysis of the fetishistic character of commodities, which was foolishly neglected in those years—presents itself as an immense accumulation of spectacles, in which all that was directly lived is distanced in a representation. The spectacle does not simply coincide, however, with the sphere of images or with what we call today the *media:* It is "a social relation among people, mediated by images," the expropriation and the alienation of human sociality itself. Or rather, using a lapidary formula, "the spectacle is capital to such a degree of accumulation that it becomes an image." But for that very reason, the spectacle is nothing but the pure form of separation: When the real world is transformed into an image and images become real, the practical power of humans is separated from itself and presented as a world unto itself. In the figure of this world separated and organized by the media, in which the forms of the State and the economy are interwoven, the mercantile economy attains the status of absolute and irresponsible sovereignty over all social life. After having falsified all of production, it can now manipulate collective perception and take control of social memory and social communication, transforming them into a single spectacular commodity where everything can be called into question except the spectacle itself, which, as such, says nothing but, "What appears is good, what is good appears."

Today, in the era of the complete triumph of the spectacle, what can be reaped from the heritage of Debord? It is clear that the spectacle is language, the very communicativity or linguistic being of humans. This means that a fuller Marxian analysis should deal with the fact that capitalism (or any other name one wants to give the process that today dominates world history) was directed not only toward the expropriation of productive activity, but also and principally toward the alienation of language itself, of the very linguistic and communicative nature of humans, of that *logos* which one of Heraclitus's fragments identified as the Common. The extreme form of this expropriation of the Common is the spectacle, that is, the politics we live in. But this also means that in the spectacle our own linguistic nature comes back to us inverted. This is why (precisely because what is being expropriated is the very possibility of a common good) the violence of the spectacle is so destructive; but for the same reason the spectacle retains something like a positive possibility that can be used against it.

This condition is very similar to what the cabalists called "the isolation of the Shekinah" and attributed to Aher, one of the four rabbis who, according to a celebrated Haggadah of the Talmud, entered into Pardes (that is, into supreme knowledge). "Four rabbis," the story says, "entered Paradise: Ben Azzai, Ben Zoma, Aher and Rabbi Akiba....Ben Azzai cast a glance and died....Ben Zoma looked and went mad....Aher cut off the twigs...Rabbi Akiba left unharmed."

The Shekinah is the last of the ten Sefirot or attributes of the divinity, the one that expresses the very presence of the divine, its manifestation or habitation on earth: its "word." Aher's "cutting off the twigs" is identified by the cabalists with the sin of Adam, who instead of contemplating all of the Sefirot chose to contemplate the final one, isolating it from the others and in this way separating the tree of knowledge from the tree of life. Like Adam, Aher represents humanity insofar as, making knowledge his own destiny and his own specific power, he isolates knowledge and the word, which are nothing but the most complete form of the manifestation of God (the Shekinah), from the other Sefirot in which God is revealed. *The risk here is that the word—that is, the non-latency and the revelation of something (anything whatsoever)—be separated from what it reveals and acquire an autonomous consistency.* Revealed and manifested (and hence common and shareable) being is separated from the thing revealed and stands between it and humans. In this condition of exile, the Shekinah loses its positive power and becomes harmful (the cabalists said that it "sucked the milk of evil").

This is the sense in which the isolation of the Shekinah expresses the condition of our era. Whereas under the old regime the estrangement of the communicative essence of humans took the form of a presupposition that served as a common foundation, in the society of spectacle it is this very communicativity, this generic essence itself (i.e., language), that is separated in an autonomous sphere. What hampers communication is communicability itself; humans are separated by what unites them. Journalists and mediacrats are the new priests of this alienation from human linguistic nature.

In the society of spectacle, in fact, the isolation of the Shekinah reaches its final phase, where language is not only constituted in an autonomous sphere, but also no longer even reveals anything—or better, it reveals the nothingness of all things. There is nothing of God, of the world, or of the revealed in language. In this extreme nullifying unveiling, however, language (the linguistic nature of humans) remains once again hidden and separated, and thus, one last time, in its unspoken power, it dooms humans to a historical era and a State: the era of the spectacle, or of accomplished nihilism. This is why today power founded on a presupposed foundation is tottering all over the globe and the kingdoms of the earth set course, one after another, for the democratic-spectacular regime that constitutes the completion of the State-form. Even more than economic necessity and technological development, what drives the nations of the earth toward a single common destiny is the alienation from linguistic being, the uprooting of all peoples from their vital dwelling in language.

For this very reason, however, the era in which we live is also that in which for the first time it is possible for humans to experience their own linguistic being—not this or that content of language, but language *itself*, not this or that true proposition, but the very fact that one speaks. Contemporary politics is this devastating *experimentum linguae* that all over the planet unhinges and empties traditions and beliefs, ideologies and religions, identities and communities.

Only those who succeed in carrying it to completion— without allowing what reveals to remain veiled in the nothingness that reveals, but bringing language itself to language—will be the first citizens of a community with neither presuppositions nor a State, where the nullifying and determining power of what is common will be pacified and where the Shekinah will have stopped sucking the evil milk of its own separation.

Like Rabbi Akiba, they will enter into the paradise of language and leave unharmed.

x i x

Tiananmen

WHAT COULD be the politics of whatever singularity, that is, of a being whose community is mediated not by any condition of belonging (being red, being Italian, being Communist) nor by the simple absence of conditions (a negative community, such as that recently proposed in France by Maurice Blanchot), but by belonging itself? A herald from Beijing carries the elements of a response.

What was most striking about the demonstrations of the Chinese May was the relative absence of determinate contents in their demands (democracy and freedom are notions too generic and broadly defined to constitute the real object of a conflict, and the only concrete demand, the rehabilitation of Hu Yao-Bang, was immediately granted). This makes the violence of the State's reaction seem even more inexplicable. It is likely, however, that the disproportion is only apparent and that the Chinese leaders acted, from their point of view, with greater lucidity than the Western observers who were exclusively concerned with advancing increasingly less plausible arguments about the opposition between democracy and communism.

The novelty of the coming politics is that it will no longer be a struggle for the conquest or control of the State, but a struggle between the State and the non-State (humanity), an insurmountable disjunction between whatever singularity and the State organization. This has nothing to do with the simple affirmation of the social in opposition to the State that has often found expression in the protest movements of recent years. Whatever singularities cannot form a *societas* because they do not possess any identity to vindicate nor any bond of belonging for which to seek recognition. In the final instance the State can recognize any claim for identity—even that of a State identity within the State (the recent history of relations between the State and terrorism is an eloquent confirmation of this fact). What the State cannot tolerate in any way, however, is that the singularities form a community without affirming an identity, that humans co-belong without any representable condition of belonging (even in the form of a simple presupposition). The State, as Alain Badiou has shown, is not founded on a social bond, of which it would be the expression, but rather on the dissolution, the unbinding it prohibits. For the State, therefore, what is important is never the singularity as such, but only its inclusion in some identity, whatever identity (but the possibility of the *whatever* itself being taken up without an identity is a threat the State cannot come to terms with).

A being radically devoid of any representable identity would be absolutely irrelevant to the State. This is what, in our culture, the hypocritical dogma of the sacredness of human life and the vacuous declarations of human rights are meant to hide. *Sacred* here can only mean what the term meant in Roman law: *Sacer* was the one who had been excluded from the human world and who, even though she or he could not be sacrificed, could be killed without committing homicide ("neque fas est eum immolari, sed qui occidit parricidio non damnatur"). (It is significant from this perspective that the extermination of the Jews was not conceived as homicide, neither by the executioners nor by the judges; rather, the judges presented it as a crime against humanity. The victorious powers tried to compensate for this lack of identity with the concession of a State identity, which itself became the source of new massacres.)

Whatever singularity, which wants to appropriate belonging itself, its own being-in-language, and thus rejects all identity and every condition of belonging, is the principal enemy of the State. Wherever these singularities peacefully demonstrate their being in common there will be a Tiananmen, and, sooner or later, the tanks will appear.

Appendix: The Irreparable

Preface

These fragments can be read as a commentary on section 9 of Martin Heidegger's *Being and Time* and proposition 6.44 of Ludwig Wittgenstein's
Tractatus. Both texts deal with the attempt to define an old problem of
metaphysics: the relationship between essence and existence, between *quid
est* and *quod est*. Whether and to what extent these fragments, even with
their obvious shortcomings, do succeed in furthering our thought about this
relationship, which the meager propensity of our times for ontology (first
philosophy) has hastily left aside, will be clear only if one can situate them
in this context.

The Irreparable is that things are just as they are, in this or that mode, consigned without remedy to their way of being. States of things are irreparable, whatever they may be: sad or happy, atrocious or blessed. How you are, how the world is—this is the Irreparable.

Revelation does not mean revelation of the sacredness of the world, but only revelation of its irreparably profane character. (The name always and only names things.) Revelation consigns the world to profanation and thingness—and isn't this precisely what has happened? The possibility of salvation begins only at this point; it is the salvation of the profanity of the world, of its being-thus.

(This is why those who try to make the world and life sacred again are just as impious as those who despair about its profanation. This is why Protestant theology, which clearly separates the profane world from the divine, is both wrong and right: right because the world has been consigned irrevocably by revelation [by language] to the profane sphere; wrong because it will be saved precisely insofar as it is profane.)

The world—insofar as it is absolutely, irreparably profane—is God.

According to Spinoza the two forms of the irreparable, confidence or safety (*securitas*) and despair (*desperatio*), are identical from this point of view (*Ethics*, III, Definitions XIV and XV). What is essential is only that every cause of doubt has been removed, that things are certainly and definitively thus; it does not matter whether this brings joy or sadness. As a state of things, heaven is perfectly equivalent to hell even though it has the opposite sign. (But if we could feel confident in despair, or desperate in confidence, then we would be able to perceive in the state of things a margin, a limbo that cannot be contained within it.)

The root of all pure joy and sadness is that the world is as it is. Joy or sadness that arises because the world is not what it seems or what we want it to be is impure or provisional. But in the highest degree of their purity, in the *so be it* said to the world when every legitimate cause of doubt and hope has been removed, sadness and joy refer not to negative or positive qualities, but to a pure *being-thus* without any attributes.

The proposition that God is not revealed *in* the world could also be expressed by the following statement: What is properly divine is that the world does not reveal God. (Hence this is not the "bitterest" proposition of the *Tractatus*.)

The world of the happy and that of the unhappy, the world of the good and that of the evil contain the same states of things; with respect to their being-thus they are perfectly identical. The just person does not reside in another world. The one who is saved and the one who is lost have the same arms and legs. The glorious body cannot but be the mortal body itself. What changes are not the things but their limits. It is as if there hovered over them something like a halo, a glory.

The Irreparable is neither an essence nor an existence, neither a substance nor a quality, neither a possibility nor a necessity. It is not properly a modality of being, but it is the being that is always already given in modality, that *is* its modalities. It is not *thus*, but rather it is *its* thus.

∎

Thus. The meaning of this little word is the most difficult to grasp. "Hence things stand thus." But would we say of an animal that its world is thus-and-thus? Even if we could exactly describe the animal's world, representing it as the animal sees it (as in the color illustrations of Uexküll's books that depict the world of the bee, the hermit crab, and the fly), certainly that world would still not contain the *thus*; it would not be *thus* for the animal: It would not be irreparable.

Being-thus is not a substance of which *thus* would express a determination or a qualification. Being is not a presupposition that is before or after its qualities. Being that is irreparably thus *is* its *thus*; it is only its mode of being. (The thus is not an essence that determines an existence, but it finds its essence in its own being-thus, in its being its own determination.)

Thus means not otherwise. (This leaf is green; hence it is neither red nor yellow.) But can one conceive of a being-thus that negates all possibilities, every predicate—that is, only the *thus*, such as it is, and no other way? This would be the only correct way to understand negative theology: neither this nor that, neither thus nor thus—but thus, as it is, with all its predicates (all its predicates is not a predicate). *Not otherwise* negates each predicate as a property (on the plane of essence), but takes them up again as im-properties or improprieties (on the plane of existence).

     (Such a being would be a pure, singular and yet perfectly whatever existence.)

     As anaphora, the term *thus* refers back to a preceding term, and only through this preceding term does it (which, in itself, has no meaning) identify its proper referent.

     Here, however, we have to conceive of an anaphora that no longer refers back to any meaning or any referent, an absolute *thus* that does not presuppose anything, that is completely exposed.

     The two characteristics that according to grammarians define the meaning of the pronoun, ostension and relation, *deixis* and ana-phora, have to be completely rethought here. The mode in which these characteristics have been understood has determined the theory of being, that is, first philosophy, since its origins.

     Pure being (the *substantia sine qualitate*), which is in question in the pronoun, has constantly been understood according to the schema of presupposition. In ostension, through language's capacity to refer to the instance of discourse taking place, what is presupposed is the immediate being-there of a non-linguistic element, which language cannot say but only show (hence showing has provided the model for existence and denotation, the Aristotelian *tode ti*). In anaphora, through reference to a term already mentioned in discourse, this presupposition is posited in relation to language as the subject (*hypokeimenon*) that carries what is said (hence anaphora has provided the model for essence and meaning, the Aristotelian *ti hen einai*). The pronoun, through *deixis*, presupposes relationless being and, through anaphora, makes that being "the subject" of discourse. Thus anaphora presupposes ostension, and ostension refers back to anaphora (insofar as *deixis* presupposes an instance of discourse): They imply each other. (This is the origin of the double meaning of the term *ousia:* the single ineffable individual and the substance underlying its predicates.)

The originary fracture of being in essence and existence, meaning and denotation is thus expressed in the double meaning of the pronoun, without the relationship between these terms ever coming to light as such. What needs to be conceived here is precisely this relation that is neither denotation nor meaning, neither ostension nor anaphora, but rather their reciprocal implication. It is not the non-linguistic, the relationless object of a pure ostension, nor is it this object's being in language as that which is said in the proposition; rather, it is the being-in-language-of-the-non-linguistic, the thing itself. In other words, it is not the presupposition of a being, but its exposure.

The expositive relationship between existence and essence, between denotation and meaning, is not a relationship of identity (the same thing, *idem*), but of ipseity (the same thing, *ipsum*). Many misunderstandings in philosophy have arisen from the confusion of the one with the other. The thing of thought is not the identity, but the thing *itself*. The latter is not another thing toward which the thing tends, transcending itself, but neither is it simply the same thing. The thing here transcends toward *itself*, toward its own being such as it is.

As such.[3] Here the anaphora "as" does not refer to a preceding referential term (to a prelinguistic substance), and "such" does not serve to indicate a referent that gives "as" its meaning. "Such" has no other existence than "as," and "as" has no other essence than "such." They stipulate each other, they expose one another, and what exists is being-such, an absolute such-quality that does not refer back to any presupposition. *Arché anypothetos*. (The anaphoric relation is played out here between the named thing and its being named, between the name and its reference to the thing: between, that is, the name "rose" insofar as it signifies the rose and the rose insofar as it is signified by the name "rose." The space of the anaphoric relation is solely contained in this interworld.)

Assuming my being-such, my manner of being, is not assuming this or that quality, this or that character, virtue or vice, wealth or poverty. My qualities and my being-thus are not qualifications of a substance (of a subject) that remains behind them and that I would truly be. I am never *this* or *that*, but always *such*, *thus*. *Eccum sic:* absolutely. Not possession but limit, not presupposition but exposure.

Exposure, in other words being such-as, is not any of the real predicates (being red, hot, small, smooth, etc.), but neither is it other than these (otherwise it would be something else added to the concept of a thing and therefore still a real predicate). That you are exposed is not one of your qualities, but neither is it other than them (we could say, in fact, that it is none-other than them). Whereas real predicates express relationships within language, exposure is pure relationship with language itself, with its taking-place. It is what happens to something (or more precisely, to the taking-place of something) by the very fact of being in relation to language, the fact of being-called. A thing is (called) red and by virtue of this, insofar as it is *called* such and refers to itself as *such* (not simply as red), it is exposed. Existence as exposure is the being-*as* of a *such*. (The category of *suchness* is, in this sense, the fundamental category that remains unthought in every quality.)

To exist means to take on qualities, to submit to the torment of being such (*inqualieren*). Hence quality, the being-such of each thing, is its torture and its source—its limit. How you are—your face—is your torture and your source. And each being is and must be its mode of being, its manner of rising forth: being *such* as it is.

The *such* does not presuppose the *as*; it exposes it, it is its taking-place. (Only in this sense can we say that essence lies—*liegt*—in existence.) The *as* does not suppose the *such*; it is its exposure, its being pure exteriority. (Only in this sense can we say that essence envelops— *involvit*—existence.)

Language says something as something: the tree as "tree," the house as "house." Thought has been concentrated either on the first something (existence, that something is) or on the second (essence, what something is), either on their identity or their difference. But what really has to be thought—the word "as," the relation of exposure—has remained unthought. This originary "as" is the theme of philosophy, the thing of thought.

Heidegger brought to light the structure of the word *als*, "as," "insofar as," that characterizes apophantic judgment. Apophantic judgment is founded on "insofar as" as the circular structure of comprehension. Comprehension comprehends and discovers something always already on the basis of something and insofar as it is something, retreating, so to speak, toward that in which it was already lodged. In judgment this structure of "something insofar as it is something" takes the form familiar to us as the subject-predicate relation. The judgment "the chalk is white" says the chalk insofar as it is white and, in this way, hides the around-and-about-which in the insofar-as-it-is-something through which the former is understood.

But the structure and the meaning of the *als*, the "as," are still not clear. By saying something as "something," what is hidden is not only the around-and-about-which (the first thing) but primarily the *as* itself. The thinking that tries to grasp being *as* being retreats toward the entity without adding to it any further determination, but also without presupposing it in an ostension as the ineffable subject of the predication; comprehending it in its being-such, in the midst of its *as*, it grasps its pure non-latency, its pure exteriority. It no longer says *something* as "*something*," but brings to speech the *as* itself.

Meaning and denotation do not account for all of linguistic signification. We have to introduce a third term: the thing itself, the being-such, that is neither what is denoted nor what is meant. (This is the meaning of the Platonic theory of ideas.)

Neither the being that is absolutely not posited and relationless (*athesis*), nor the being that is posited, related, and factitious, but an eternal exposure and facticity: *aeisthesis*, an eternal sensation.

A being that is never itself, but is only the existent. It is never existent, but it *is* the existent, completely and without refuge. It neither founds nor directs nor nullifies the existent; it is only its being exposed, its nimbus, its limit. The existent no longer refers back to being; it is in the midst of being, and being is entirely abandoned in the existent. Without refuge and nonetheless safe—safe in its being irreparable.

Being, which is the existent, is forever safe from the risk of itself existing as a thing or of being nothing. The existent, abandoned in the midst of being, is perfectly exposed.

Atticus defines the idea as "*paraitia tou einai toiauta ecasth' oiaper esti*," for each thing, not cause but *paracause*, and not simply for being, but for being-such-as-it-is.

The being-such of each thing is the idea. It is as if the form, the knowability, the features of every entity were detached from it, not as another thing, but as an *intentio*, an angel, an image. The mode of being of this *intentio* is neither a simple existence nor a transcendence; it is a paraexistence or a paratranscendence that dwells beside the thing (in all the sense of the prefix "para-"), so close that it *almost* merges with it, giving it a halo. It is not the identity of the thing and yet it is nothing other than the thing (it is *none-other*). The existence of the idea is, in other words, a paradigmatic existence: the manifesting beside itself of each thing (*para-deigma*). But this showing beside itself is a limit—or rather, it is the unraveling, the indetermination of a limit: a halo.

(This is a Gnostic reading of the Platonic idea. It also applies to the angels-intelligences in Avicenna and the love poets, and to Origen's *eidos* and the radiant cloak of the *Song of the Pearl*. Salvation takes place in this irreparable image.)

An eternal as-suchness: This is the idea.

III

Redemption is not an event in which what was profane becomes sacred and what was lost is found again. Redemption is, on the contrary, the irreparable loss of the lost, the definitive profanity of the profane. But, precisely for this reason, they now reach their end—the advent of a limit.

We can have hope only in what is without remedy. That things are thus and thus—this is still in the world. But that this is irreparable, that this *thus* is without remedy, that we can contemplate it as such—this is the only passage outside the world. (The innermost character of salvation is that we are saved only at the point when we no longer want to be. At this point, there is salvation—but not for us.)

Being-thus, being one's own mode of being—we cannot grasp this as a thing. It is precisely the evacuation of any thingness. (This is why Indian logicians said that *sicceitas*, the being-thus of things, was nothing but their being deprived of any proper nature, their vacuity, and that between the world and Nirvana there is not the slightest difference.)

The human is the being that, bumping into things and

only in this encounter, opens up to the non-thinglike. And inversely, the human is the one that, being open to the non-thinglike, is, for this very reason, irreparably consigned to things.

Non-thingness (spirituality) means losing oneself in things, losing oneself to the point of not being able to conceive of anything but things, and only then, in the experience of the irremediable thingness of the world, bumping into a limit, touching it. (This is the meaning of the word "exposure.")

The taking-place of things does not take place in the world. Utopia is the very topia of things.

So be it. In every thing affirm simply the *thus*, *sic*, beyond good and evil. But *thus* does not simply mean in this or that mode, with those certain properties. "So be it" means "let the thus be." In other words, it means "yes."

(This is the meaning of Nietzsche's yes. The yes is said not simply of a state of things, but of its being-*thus*. Only for this reason can it eternally return. The *thus* is eternal.)

The being-thus of each thing is, in this sense, incorruptible. (This is precisely the meaning of Origen's theory that what returns is not corporeal substance but *eidos*.)

Dante classifies human languages by their way of saying yes: *oc, oil, sí*. Yes, *thus*, is the name of language, it expresses its meaning: the being-in-language-of-the-non-linguistic. But the existence of language is the yes said to the world so that it remains suspended over the nothingness of language.

In the principle of reason ("There is a reason why there is something rather than nothing"), what is essential is neither *that something is* (being) nor *that something is not* (nothingness), but that something is *rather* than nothingness. For this reason it cannot be read simply as an opposition between two terms—*is/is not*. It also contains a third term: the *rather* (which is related to the Old English "rathe" meaning quick or eager, and which in Latin is *potius*, from *potis*, that which is able), the power to not not-be.

(What is astonishing is not that something was able to be, but that it was able to not not-be.)

The principle of reason can be expressed in this way:

Language (reason) is that whereby something exists rather (*potius*, more powerfully) than nothing. Language opens the possibility of not-being, but at the same time it also opens a stronger possibility: existence, that something is. What the principle properly says, however, is that existence is not an inert fact, that a *potius*, a power inheres in it. But this is not a potentiality to be that is opposed to a potentiality to not-be (who would decide between these two?); it is a potentiality to not not-be. The contingent is not simply the non-necessary, that which can not-be, but that which, being the *thus*, being only its mode of being, is capable of the *rather*, can not not-be. (Being-thus is not contingent; it is necessarily contingent. Nor is it necessary; it is contingently necessary.)

"An affect toward a thing we imagine to be free is greater than that toward a thing we imagine to be necessary, and consequently is still greater than that toward a thing we imagine as possible or contingent. But imagining a thing as free can be nothing but simply imagining it while we are ignorant of the causes by which it has been determined to act. Therefore, an affect toward a thing we imagine simply is, other things equal, greater than that toward a thing we imagine as necessary, possible, or contingent. Hence, it is the greatest of all" (Spinoza, *Ethics*, Part V, Proposition 5, Demonstration).

Seeing something simply in its being-thus — irreparable, but not for that reason necessary; thus, but not for that reason contingent — is love.

At the point you perceive the irreparability of the world, at that point it is transcendent.

How the world is — this is outside the world.

Translator's Notes

1. Whatever (*qualunque*). This adjective-pronoun has many uses in Italian that are rather awkward in English. The thematic centrality of the term, however, has required that we preserve its position every time it occurs in the text. The corresponding French term (*quelconque*) has a resonance in the work of other contemporary philosophers, such as Gilles Deleuze and Alain Badiou, that unfortunately may be lost on English readers because various translations have rendered it differently, as "particular" in some cases and "general" in others. As Agamben makes clear, however, "whatever" (*qualunque* or *quelconque*) refers precisely to that which is neither particular nor general, neither individual nor generic.

2. Agamben translates Russell's term "any" into Italian as *qualunque* (whatever), but when translating back into English we had to restore Russell's original terminology. The English usage of "any" and "whatever" is very close, however, and should be kept in mind throughout this passage. Agamben's reference here is to Russell's essay "Mathematical Logic as Based on the Theory of Types" (1908), which appears in *Logic and Knowledge* (London: Unwin Hyman, 1956), pp. 57–102; see in particular section II, "All and Any," pp. 64–69.

3. As such (*tale quale*). We use the standard English translation of this phrase, "as such," but unfortunately, with this decision we lose the conceptual relationship in this section between *quale* (rendered here as "such") and *qualunque* (whatever). (The reader may find it useful to keep in mind the corresponding French term, *tel quel*.)

Giorgio Agamben
teaches philosophy at both the
Collège International de Philosophie in Paris and the University of Macerata in Italy.
He has written numerous books,
two of which have been published in translation by the
University of Minnesota Press:
Language and Death: The Place of Negativity
(1991) and
Stanzas: Word and Phantasm in Western Culture
(1992).

Michael Hardt
is the author of
Gilles Deleuze: An Apprenticeship in Philosophy
(Minnesota, 1993),
the translator of Antonio Negri's
The Savage Anomaly:
The Power of Spinoza's Metaphysics and Politics
(Minnesota, 1990),
and the cotranslator (with Karen Pinkus) of Giorgio Agamben's
Language and Death: The Place of Negativity
(Minnesota, 1991).